# Mass Blasters

by Melanie Joyce

illustrated by Janos Jantner

## Titles in the Travellers series

**Level 3**

| | |
|---|---|
| Goal! | Jane A C West |
| Too Hot | Roger Hurn/Alison Hawes |

**Level 4**

| | |
|---|---|
| A Big Catch | Alison Hawes |
| Deyda's Drum | Roger Hurn |
| The Strawberry Thief | Alison Hawes |
| Billy's Boy | Melanie Joyce |

**Level 5**

| | |
|---|---|
| Cage Boy | Jillian Powell |
| Master Blasters | Melanie Joyce |
| Game Player King | Stan Cullimore |
| In the Zone | Tony Norman |

**Level 6**

| | |
|---|---|
| Dodgems | Jane A C West |
| Tansy Smith | Helen Orme |

**Level 7**

| | |
|---|---|
| Pirate Attack | Jonny Zucker |
| Hitting the Basket | Jonny Zucker |

Badger Publishing Limited
Oldmedow Road, Hardwick Industrial Estate,
King's Lynn PE30 4JJ
Telephone: 01438 791037
www.badgerlearning.co.uk

8 10 9 7

Master Blasters ISBN 978 1 84691 849 0

Publisher: David Jamieson
Editor: Danny Pearson
Design: Fiona Grant
Illustration: Janos Jantner

# Master Blasters

## Contents

Badger
LEARNING

## Vocabulary

Diwali          Rocket          Building

Competition     Dropped         Firework

Landed          Exploded        Ran

Crew

## Main characters

Malika lives in Pakistan with her Mum.
Her Dad works away in England and
Malika misses him. Imran is Malika's
friend.

# Diwali

Diwali is a festival in Hinduism, Sikhism, Buddhism, and Jainism religions.

The five day festival of Diwali occurs on the new moon between October 13 and November 14.

People decorate their homes with lights, and lots of fireworks are used during the celebrations.

On the day of Diwali, many people wear new clothes and share sweets and gifts.

Diwali is popularly known as the "festival of lights".

# Chapter 1
# The Competition

It was nearly Diwali.

Malika was building a rocket

"Is it for Diwali?" asked Imran.

"It's for a competition.

I want to win the prize money.

I want to go and see my Dad."

There was a 'WHOOSH' and lots of
smoke.

The rocket shot into the sky.

Suddenly the rocket fell.

It landed in Mr Shar's yard.

"The Diwali fireworks are in there!"

Suddenly, fireworks shot everywhere.

The noise was terrible.

People ran from their houses

# Chapter 3
# In the News

The news soon spread.

TV crews arrived.

"I'm in big trouble,"

said Malika

"It's not her fault," said Imran.

He explained about the rocket

Malika told her story on TV.

People felt sorry for her.

They sent her lots of rupees.

Malika went to see her Dad after all.

That was the best prize ever.

## Questions

Why does Malika build a rocket?

What does Imran put inside the rocket?

Where does the rocket land?

Where does Malika tell her story?

# Lifelines

## by Melanie Joyce
## illustrated by Janos Jantner

## Contents

## Vocabulary:

Travellers    Trailer    Steep

Missed    Unhappy    Promise

## Main characters:

Rosie

Dad

# Chapter 1
# The Move

Rosie's family were Travellers.

They lived in a trailer.

When Dad became ill, they moved into a house.

"When are we going home?" said Rosie.

"This is home," said Dad.

Rosie did not like the brick walls.

She did not like the steep stairs.

Rosie missed her cousins.

She missed her aunties and uncles.

That night, Rosie's bedroom was
empty.

# Chapter 2

# Searchers

Rosie was nowhere to be found.
Suddenly there was a knock at the
door.

It was the Travellers from the camp.
Rosie had gone to find them.

# Chapter 3
# The Promise

After that Dad made a promise.

"I'll buy a trailer," he said.

"In the summer we'll go away.

We will always be Travellers, Rosie."

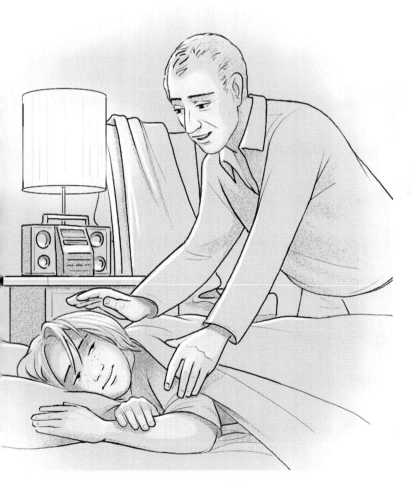

Rosie slept well that night

She dreamed of Summer and life on the road.

## Questions:

Why did the family move into a house?

What did Rosie not like about the house?

Who did Rosie miss?

What promise did Rosie get from her Dad?